MW01002007

Car Seat Blankets

Keep Baby warm and comfy when on the move! It's easy with these quick-to-knit little blankets that are just right for car seats, strollers, swings, and other carriers. All eight designs call for medium weight yarn and Easy or Easy-Plus skill levels.

LEISURE ARTS, INC. • Maumelle, Arkansas

LACE STITCH

◐■▢▷ **EASY**

Finished Size:
16¾" x 20" (42.5 cm x 51 cm)

SHOPPING LIST

Yarn (Medium Weight)
[16 ounces, 812 yards
(453.6 grams, 742 meters) per skein]:
☐ ½ skein

Knitting Needles
☐ Size 8 (5 mm) **or** size needed for gauge

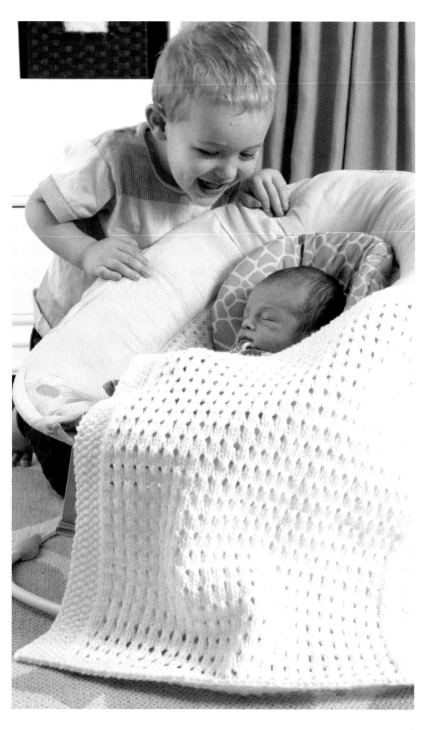

GAUGE INFORMATION

In pattern, 16 sts and 24 rows = 4" (10 cm)

TECHNIQUES USED

🎥 YO *(Fig. 3a, page 43)*
🎥 K2 tog *(Fig. 4, page 45)*

INSTRUCTIONS
Blanket

Cast on 67 sts.

Rows 1-6: K1, (P1, K1) across.

Row 7 (Right side)**:** (K1, P1) 3 times, knit across to last 6 sts, (P1, K1) 3 times.

Row 8: K1, (P1, K1) twice, purl across to last 5 sts, K1, (P1, K1) twice.

Row 9: (K1, P1) 3 times, K2, (YO, K2 tog) across to last 7 sts, K1, (P1, K1) 3 times.

Row 10: K1, (P1, K1) twice, purl across to last 5 sts, K1, (P1, K1) twice.

Row 11: (K1, P1) 3 times, knit across to last 6 sts, (P1, K1) 3 times.

Repeat Rows 8-11 for pattern until Blanket measures approximately 19" (48.5 cm) from cast on edge, ending by working Row 11.

Last 6 Rows: K1, (P1, K1) across.

Bind off all sts in pattern.

BASKET WEAVE

◖■◻◻◻ **EASY**

Finished Size:
17¾" x 21½" (45 cm x 54.5 cm)

SHOPPING LIST

Yarn (Medium Weight)
[5 ounces, 256 yards
(141 grams, 234 meters) per skein]:
☐ Green - 1 skein
☐ Yellow - 1 skein
☐ Blue - 1 skein
☐ Pink - 1 skein

Knitting Needles
☐ Size 8 (5 mm) **or** size needed for gauge

GAUGE INFORMATION

In pattern, two repeats (12 sts) = 2¾" (7 cm); 24 rows = 3¼" (8.25 cm)
In Garter Stitch,18 sts and 32 rows = 4" (10 cm)

INSTRUCTIONS
Blanket

With Pink, cast on 78 sts.

Rows 1-8: Knit across; at end of Row 8, cut Pink.

Row 9 (Right side)**:** With Blue, knit across.

Row 10: K6, (P3, K3) across to last 6 sts, P1, K5.

Rows 11-14: Repeat Rows 9 and 10 twice; at end of Row 14, cut Blue.

Row 15: With Yellow, knit across.

Row 16: K5, P1, (K3, P3) across to last 6 sts, K6.

Rows 17-20: Repeat Rows 15 and 16 twice; at end or Row 20, cut Yellow.

Row 21: With Green, knit across.

Row 22: K6, (P3, K3) across to last 6 sts, P1, K5.

Rows 23-26: Repeat Rows 21 and 22 twice; at end of Row 26, cut Green.

Row 27: With Pink, knit across.

Row 28: K5, P1, (K3, P3) across to last 6 sts, K6.

Rows 29-32: Repeat Rows 27 and 28 twice; at end of Row 32, cut Pink.

Rows 33-152: Repeat Rows 9-32, 5 times.

Rows 153-160: With Blue, knit across.

Bind off all sts in **knit**.

LACY RIPPLES

 **EASY**

Finished Size:
16¼" x 20" (41.5 cm x 51 cm)

SHOPPING LIST

Yarn (Medium Weight) **MEDIUM 4**
[4 ounces, 204 yards
(113 grams, 187 meters) per skein]:
☐ Variegated - 2 skeins
[5 ounces, 256 yards
(141 grams, 234 meters) per skein]:
☐ Green - 1 skein
☐ Yellow - 1 skein

Knitting Needles
☐ Size 8 (5 mm) **or** size needed for gauge

GAUGE INFORMATION

In pattern (Rows 10-13), two repeats (22 sts) = 5" (12.75 cm);
20 rows = 3" (7.5 cm)

TECHNIQUES USED

YO *(Fig. 3a, page 43)*
K2 tog *(Fig. 4, page 45)*
SSK *(Figs. 5a-c, page 45)*

INSTRUCTIONS

Blanket

With Variegated, cast on 76 sts.

Row 1: (K1, P1) across.

Row 2: (P1, K1) across.

Rows 3-5: Repeat Rows 1 and 2 once, then repeat Row 1 once **more**.

Row 6 (Right side): P1, (K1, P1) twice, knit across to last 4 sts,
(P1, K1) twice.

Row 7: K1, (P1, K1) twice, purl across to last 4 sts, (K1, P1) twice.

Row 8: P1, (K1, P1) twice, ★ SSK twice, YO, (K1, YO) 3 times, K2 tog twice; repeat from ★ across to last 5 sts, K1, (P1, K1) twice.

Row 9: (K1, P1) twice, knit across to last 5 sts, P1, (K1, P1) twice.

Row 10: P1, (K1, P1) twice, knit across to last 4 sts, (P1, K1) twice.

Row 11: K1, (P1, K1) twice, purl across to last 4 sts, (K1, P1) twice.

Row 12: P1, (K1, P1) twice, ★ SSK twice, YO, (K1, YO) 3 times, K2 tog twice; repeat from ★ across to last 5 sts, K1, (P1, K1) twice.

Row 13: (K1, P1) twice, knit across to last 5 sts, P1, (K1, P1) twice.

Cut Variegated.

Rows 14-17: With Green, repeat Rows 10-13.

Cut Green.

Rows 18-21: With Yellow, repeat Rows 10-13.

Cut Yellow.

With Variegated, repeat Rows 10-13 for pattern until Blanket measures approximately 16½" (42 cm) from cast on edge, ending by working Row 13.

Cut Variegated.

Next 4 Rows: With Yellow, repeat Rows 10-13.

Cut Yellow.

Next 4 Rows: With Green, repeat Rows 10-13.

Cut Green.

Next 10 Rows: With Variegated, repeat Rows 10-13 twice, then repeat Rows 10 and 11 once **more**.

Next Row: (P1, K1) across.

Last 4 Rows: Repeat Rows 1-4.

Bind off all sts in pattern.

LACE CHEVRONS

◖■□▭ EASY

Finished Size:
16½" x 20" (42 cm x 51 cm)

SHOPPING LIST

Yarn (Medium Weight)
[7 ounces, 364 yards
(198 grams, 333 meters) per skein]:
☐   Yellow - 1 skein
☐   Green - 1 skein
[5 ounces, 244 yards
(141 grams, 223 meters) per skein]:
☐   Variegated - 1 skein

Knitting Needles
☐   Size 8 (5 mm) **or** size needed for gauge

GAUGE INFORMATION

In Seed Stitch, 16 sts and 20 rows = 4" (10 cm)
One Lace pattern (15 sts) = 3½" (9 cm)
In Stockinette Stitch, 17 sts and 22 rows = 4" (10 cm)

TECHNIQUES USED

YO (*Fig. 3a, page 43*)
K2 tog (*Fig. 4, page 45*)
SSK (*Figs. 5a-c, page 45*)

INSTRUCTIONS

Blanket

With Yellow, cast on 70 sts.

Rows 1 and 2: Knit across.

Row 3 (Right side)**:** Purl across.

Row 4: Knit across; cut Yellow.

Row 5: With Green, knit across.

Row 6: K1, (P1, K1) twice, purl across to last 5 sts, K1, (P1, K1) twice.

Row 7: (K1, P1) twice, K6, † (SSK, YO) 3 times, K3, (YO, K2 tog) 3 times †, K 20, repeat from † to † once, K6, (P1, K1) twice.

Row 8: K1, (P1, K1) twice, purl across to last 5 sts, K1, (P1, K1) twice.

Row 9: (K1, P1) twice, K6, † SSK, K1, YO, (SSK, YO) twice, K1, YO, (K2 tog, YO) twice, K1, K2 tog †, K 20, repeat from † to † once, K6, (P1, K1) twice.

Row 10: K1, (P1, K1) twice, purl across to last 5 sts, K1, (P1, K1) twice.

Row 11: (K1, P1) twice, K6, † SSK, K2, YO, SSK, YO, K3, YO, K2 tog, YO, K2, K2 tog †, K 20, repeat from † to † once, K6, (P1, K1) twice.

Row 12: K1, (P1, K1) twice, purl across to last 5 sts, K1, (P1, K1) twice.

Row 13: (K1, P1) twice, K6, † SSK, K3, YO, SSK, YO, K1, YO, K2 tog, YO, K3, K2 tog †, K 20, repeat from † to † once, K6, (P1, K1) twice.

Row 14: K1, (P1, K1) twice, purl across to last 5 sts, K1, (P1, K1) twice.

Row 15: (K1, P1) twice, K6, † SSK, K4, YO, SSK, YO, K1, YO, K4, K2 tog †, K 20, repeat from † to † once, K6, (P1, K1) twice.

Row 16: K1, (P1, K1) twice, purl across to last 5 sts, K1, (P1, K1) twice.

Row 17: (K1, P1) twice, K6, † SSK, K5, YO, K1, YO, K5, K2 tog †, K 20, repeat from † to † once, K6, (P1, K1) twice.

Row 18: K1, (P1, K1) twice, purl across to last 5 sts, K1, (P1, K1) twice; cut Green.

Rows 19 and 20: With Yellow, knit across.

Row 21: Purl across.

Row 22: Knit across; cut Yellow.

Row 23: With Variegated, knit across.

Row 24: K1, (P1, K1) twice, purl across to last 5 sts, K1, (P1, K1) twice.

Row 25: (K1, P1) twice, K6, † (SSK, YO) 3 times, K3, (YO, K2 tog) 3 times †, K 20, repeat from † to † once, K6, (P1, K1) twice.

Row 26: K1, (P1, K1) twice, purl across to last 5 sts, K1, (P1, K1) twice.

Row 27: (K1, P1) twice, K6, † SSK, K1, YO, (SSK, YO) twice, K1, YO, (K2 tog, YO) twice, K1, K2 tog †, K 20, repeat from † to † once, K6, (P1, K1) twice.

Row 28: K1, (P1, K1) twice, purl across to last 5 sts, K1, (P1, K1) twice.

Row 29: (K1, P1) twice, K6, † SSK, K2, YO, SSK, YO, K3, YO, K2 tog, YO, K2, K2 tog †, K 20, repeat from † to † once, K6, (P1, K1) twice.

Row 30: K1, (P1, K1) twice, purl across to last 5 sts, K1, (P1, K1) twice.

Row 31: (K1, P1) twice, K6, † SSK, K3, YO, SSK, YO, K1, YO, K2 tog, YO, K3, K2 tog †, K 20, repeat from † to † once, K6, (P1, K1) twice.

Row 32: K1, (P1, K1) twice, purl across to last 5 sts, K1, (P1, K1) twice.

Row 33: (K1, P1) twice, K6, † SSK, K4, YO, SSK, YO, K1, YO, K4, K2 tog †, K 20, repeat from † to † once, K6, (P1, K1) twice.

Row 34: K1, (P1, K1) twice, purl across to last 5 sts, K1, (P1, K1) twice.

Row 35: (K1, P1) twice, K6, † SSK, K5, YO, K1, YO, K5, K2 tog †, K 20, repeat from † to † once, K6, (P1, K1) twice.

Row 36: K1, (P1, K1) twice, purl across to last 5 sts, K1, (P1, K1) twice; cut Variegated.

Rows 37 and 38: With Yellow, knit across.

Row 39: Purl across.

Repeat Rows 4-39 for pattern until Blanket measures approximately 20" (51 cm) from cast on edge, ending by working Row 21 or Row 39.

Last Row: Knit across.

Bind off all sts in **knit**.

PRIMARY STRIPES

 **EASY**

Finished Size:
16" x 19" (40.5 cm x 48.5 cm)

SHOPPING LIST

Yarn (Medium Weight) 🧶**4**
[3.5 ounces, 190 yards
(100 grams, 174 meters) per skein]:
- ☐ White - 1 skein
- ☐ Blue - 1 skein
- ☐ Green - 1 skein
- ☐ Yellow - 1 skein
- ☐ Orange - 1 skein
- ☐ Red - 1 skein

Knitting Needles
- ☐ Size 10 (6 mm) **or** size needed for gauge

GAUGE INFORMATION

In pattern, 12 rows = 2" (5 cm)
In Stockinette Stitch, 15 sts and 20 rows = 4" (10 cm)
In Garter Stitch, 16 sts = 4" (10 cm); 20 rows = 3¾" (9.5 cm)

TECHNIQUE USED

Slip 1 as if to knit *(Fig. 1, page 42)*

INSTRUCTIONS
Blanket

With White, cast on 60 sts.

Rows 1-4: Slip 1 as if to **knit**, knit across; at end of Row 4, cut White.

Row 5 (Right side)**:** Slip 1 as if to **knit**, with Blue, knit across.

Row 6: Slip 1 as if to **knit**, K5, purl across to last 6 sts, K6.

Rows 7-12: Repeat Rows 5 and 6, 3 times; at end of Row 12, cut Blue.

Rows 13-16: Slip 1 as if to **knit**, with White, knit across; at end of Row 16, cut White.

Rows 17-24: With Green, repeat Rows 5 and 6, 4 times; at end of Row 24, cut Green.

Rows 25-28: Slip 1 as if to **knit**, with White, knit across; at end of Row 28, cut White.

Rows 29-36: With Yellow, repeat Rows 5 and 6, 4 times; at end of Row 36, cut Yellow.

Rows 37-40: Slip 1 as if to **knit**, with White, knit across; at end of Row 40, cut White.

Rows 41-48: With Orange, repeat Rows 5 and 6, 4 times; at end of Row 48, cut Orange.

Rows 49-52: Slip 1 as if to **knit**, with White, knit across; at end of Row 52, cut White.

Rows 53-60: With Red, repeat Rows 5 and 6, 4 times; at end of Row 60, cut Red.

Rows 61-64: Slip 1 as if to **knit**, with White, knit across; at end of Row 64, cut White.

Rows 65-72: With Orange, repeat Rows 5 and 6, 4 times; at end of Row 72, cut Orange.

Rows 73-76: Slip 1 as if to **knit**, with White, knit across; at end of Row 76, cut White.

Rows 77-84: With Yellow, repeat Rows 5 and 6, 4 times; at end of Row 84, cut Yellow.

Rows 85-88: Slip 1 as if to **knit**, with White, knit across; at end of Row 88, cut White.

Rows 89-96: With Green, repeat Rows 5 and 6, 4 times; at end of Row 96, cut Green.

Rows 97-100: Slip 1 as if to **knit**, with White, knit across; at end of Row 100, cut White.

Rows 101-108: With Blue, repeat Rows 5 and 6, 4 times; at end of Row 108, cut Blue.

Rows 109-112: Slip 1 as if to **knit**, with White, knit across.

Bind off all sts in **knit**.

RIBBED CHEVRON

◖■◻◻⊃ EASY +

Finished Size:
16½" x 20" (42 cm x 51 cm)

SHOPPING LIST

Yarn (Medium Weight)
[6 ounces, 315 yards
(170 grams, 288 meters) per skein]:
☐ 1 skein

Knitting Needles
☐ Size 9 (5.5 mm) **or** size needed for gauge

GAUGE INFORMATION

In pattern (Rows 9 and 10), two repeats (24 sts) = 4¼" (10.75 cm);
   20 rows = 3¾" (9.5 cm)
In Garter Stitch, 17 sts and 30 rows = 4" (10 cm)

TECHNIQUES USED

- tbl *(Fig. 2, page 42)*
- YO *(Fig. 3a, page 43)*
- K2 tog *(Fig. 4, page 45)*
- SSK *(Figs. 5a-c, page 45)*
- Slip 2 tog as if to **knit**, K1, P2SSO *(Figs. 6a & b, page 46)*

INSTRUCTIONS
Blanket

Cast on 85 sts.

Rows 1-8: Knit across.

Row 9 (Right side)**:** K6, K2 tog, K4, (K, YO, K tbl) **all** in next st, K4, ★ slip 2 tog as if to **knit**, K1, P2SSO, K4, (K, YO, K tbl) **all** in next st, K4; repeat from ★ across to last 8 sts, SSK, K6.

Row 10: K6, purl across to last 6 sts, K6.

Repeat Rows 9 and 10 for pattern until Blanket measures approximately 19" (48.5 cm) from cast on edge, ending by working a **purl** row.

Last 8 Rows: Knit across.

Bind off all sts in **knit**.

RECTANGLES

■■□□ **EASY**

Finished Size:
17½" x 20" (44.5 cm x 51 cm)

SHOPPING LIST

Yarn (Medium Weight)
[3.5 ounces, 197 yards
(100 grams, 180 meters) per skein]:
☐ 2 skeins

Knitting Needles
☐ Size 8 (5 mm) **or** size needed for gauge

GAUGE INFORMATION

In pattern (Rows 10-27), one repeat (22 sts) = 5¼" (13.25 cm);
   18 rows = 3" (7.5 cm)
In Stockinette Stitch, 17 sts and 22 rows = 4" (10 cm)

TECHNIQUE USED

🎥 Slip 1 as if to **knit** *(Fig. 1, page 42)*

INSTRUCTIONS

Blanket

Cast on 74 sts.

Rows 1-9: Slip 1 as if to **knit**, knit across.

Row 10: Slip 1 as if to **knit**, K5, P 18, (K4, P 18) twice, K6.

Row 11 (Right side)**:** Slip 1 as if to **knit**, knit across.

Row 12: Slip 1 as if to **knit**, K5, P 18, (K4, P 18) twice, K6.

Rows 13-22: Repeat Rows 11 and 12, 5 times.

Rows 23-27: Slip 1 as if to **knit**, knit across.

Repeat Rows 10-27 for pattern until Blanket measures approximately 18¾" (47.5 cm) from cast on edge, ending by working Row 22.

Last 8 Rows: Slip 1 as if to **knit**, knit across.

Bind off all sts in **knit**.

STACKED CABLES

Shown on page 39.

 **EASY**

Finished Size:
17" x 20" (43 cm x 51 cm)

SHOPPING LIST

Yarn (Medium Weight) **4** MEDIUM
[16 ounces, 1,020 yards
(454 grams, 932 meters) per skein]:
☐ ¼ skein

Knitting Needles
☐ Size 8 (5 mm) **or** size needed for gauge

GAUGE INFORMATION

In pattern (Rows 9-12), two repeats (14 sts) = 3¼" (8.25 cm);
24 rows = 3¾" (9.5 cm)

TECHNIQUES USED

- Slip 1 as if to knit (*Fig. 1, page 42*)
- YO (*Figs. 3b & c, page 44*)
- P3 tog (*Fig. 7, page 46*)

INSTRUCTIONS

Blanket

Cast on 75 sts.

Rows 1-7: Slip 1 as if to **knit**, knit across.

Row 8: Slip 1 as if to **knit**, K4, purl across to last 5 sts, K5.

Row 9 (Right side)**:** Slip 1 as if to **knit**, K6, YO, P1, P3 tog, P1, ★ YO, K2, YO, P1, P3 tog, P1; repeat from ★ across to last 7 sts, YO, K7.

Row 10: Slip 1 as if to **knit**, K4, purl across to last 5 sts, K5.

Row 11: Slip 1as if to **knit**, knit across.

Row 12: Slip 1 as if to **knit**, K4, purl across to last 5 sts, K5.

Repeat Rows 9-12 for pattern, until Blanket measures approximately 19" (48.5 cm) from cast on edge, ending by working Row 10.

Last 7 Rows: Slip 1 as if to **knit**, knit across.

Bind off all sts in **knit**.

GENERAL INSTRUCTIONS

ABBREVIATIONS

cm	centimeters
K	knit
mm	millimeters
P	purl
P2SSO	pass 2 slipped stitches over
SSK	slip, slip, knit
st(s)	stitch(es)
tbl	through back loop
tog	together
YO	yarn over

SYMBOLS & TERMS

★ — work instructions following ★ as many **more** times as indicated in addition to the first time.

† to † — work all instructions from first † to second † **as many** times as specified.

( ) or [ ] — work enclosed instructions **as many** times as specified by the number immediately following **or** work all enclosed instructions the stitch indicated **or** contains explanatory remarks.

colon (:) — the number(s) given after a colon at the end of a row denote(s) the number of stitches you should have on that row.

KNIT TERMINOLOGY

UNITED STATES		INTERNATIONAL
gauge	=	tension
bind off	=	cast off
yarn over (YO)	=	yarn forward (yfwd) **or**
		yarn around needle (yrn)

◖□□□ BEGINNER	Projects for first-time knitters using basic knit and purl stitches. Minimal shaping.
◖■□□ EASY	Projects using basic stitches, repetitive stitch patterns, simple color changes, and simple shaping and finishing.
◖■■□ INTERMEDIATE	Projects with a variety of stitches, such as basic cables and lace, simple intarsia, double-pointed needles and knitting in the round needle techniques, mid-level shaping and finishing.
◖■■■ EXPERIENCED	Projects using advanced techniques and stitches, such as short rows, fair isle, more intricate intarsia, cables, lace patterns, and numerous color changes.

KNITTING NEEDLES																		
U.S.	0	1	2	3	4	5	6	7	8	9	10	10½	11	13	15	17	19	35	50
U.K.	13	12	11	10	9	8	7	6	5	4	3	2	1	00	000	---	---	---	---
Metric - mm	2	2.25	2.75	3.25	3.5	3.75	4	4.5	5	5.5	6	6.5	8	9	10	12.75	15	19	25

Yarn Weight Symbol & Names	LACE 0	SUPER FINE 1	FINE 2	LIGHT 3	MEDIUM 4	BULKY 5	SUPER BULKY 6
Type of Yarns in Category	Fingering, size 10 crochet thread	Sock, Fingering, Baby	Sport, Baby	DK, Light Worsted	Worsted, Afghan, Aran	Chunky, Craft, Rug	Bulky, Roving
Knit Gauge Range* in Stockinette St to 4" (10 cm)	33-40** sts	27-32 sts	23-26 sts	21-24 sts	16-20 sts	12-15 sts	6-11 sts
Advised Needle Size Range	000-1	1 to 3	3 to 5	5 to 7	7 to 9	9 to 11	11 and larger

*GUIDELINES ONLY: The chart above reflects the most commonly used gauges and needle sizes for specific yarn categories.

** Lace weight yarns are usually knitted on larger needles to create lacy openwork patterns. Accordingly, a gauge range is difficult to determine. Always follow the gauge stated in your pattern.

GAUGE

Exact gauge is **essential** for proper size. Before beginning your Blanket, make a sample swatch using the yarn and needles specified in the individual instructions. After completing the swatch, measure it, counting your stitches and rows carefully. If your swatch is larger or smaller than specified, **make another, changing needle size to get the correct gauge**. Keep trying until you find the size needles that will give you the specified gauge. Once proper gauge is obtained, measure the width approximately every 3" (7.5 cm) to be sure gauge remains consistent.

SLIP 1 AS IF TO KNIT

When instructed to "slip 1 as if to **knit**," insert the right needle from **left** to **right** into the first stitch on the left needle *(Fig. 1)* and slip the stitch to the right needle.

Fig. 1

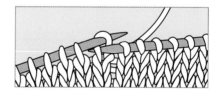

THROUGH BACK LOOP *(abbreviated tbl)*

With yarn in back, insert the right needle into the **back** of the next stitch *(Fig. 2)* from **front** to **back** and knit it.

Fig. 2

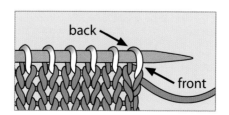

YARN OVERS

A yarn over *(abbreviated YO)* is simply placing the yarn over the right needle creating an extra stitch. Since the yarn over produces a hole in the knit fabric, it is used for a lacy effect. On the row following a yarn over, you must be careful to keep it on the needle and treat it as a stitch by knitting or purling it as instructed.

To make a yarn over, you'll loop the yarn over the needle like you would to knit or purl a stitch, bringing it either to the front or to the back of the piece so that it'll be ready to work the next stitch, creating a new stitch on the needle.

After a knit stitch, before a knit stitch
Bring the yarn forward **between** the needles, then back **over** the top of the right needle, so that it is now in position to **knit** the next stitch *(Fig. 3a)*.

Fig. 3a

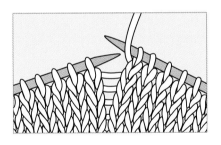

After a knit stitch, before a purl stitch

Bring the yarn forward **between** the needles, then back **over** the top of the right needle and forward **between** the needles again, so that it is now in position to **purl** the next stitch *(Fig. 3b)*.

Fig. 3b

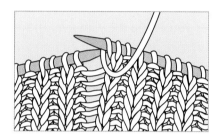

After a purl stitch, before a knit stitch

Take the yarn **over** the right needle to the back, so that it is now in position to **knit** the next stitch *(Fig. 3c)*.

Fig. 3c

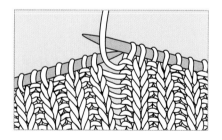

KNIT 2 TOGETHER *(abbreviated K2 tog)*

Insert the right needle into the **front** of the first two stitches on the left needle as if to **knit** *(Fig. 4)*, then **knit** them together as if they were one stitch.

Fig. 4

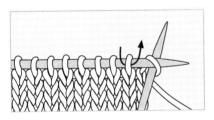

SLIP, SLIP, KNIT *(abbreviated SSK)*

With yarn in back of work, separately slip two stitches as if to **knit** *(Fig. 5a)*. Insert the **left** needle into the **front** of both slipped stitches *(Fig. 5b)* and knit them together as if they were one stitch *(Fig. 5c)*.

Fig. 5a   **Fig. 5b**

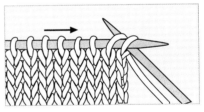

Fig. 5c

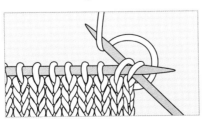

SLIP 2 TOGETHER, KNIT 1, PASS 2 SLIPPED STITCHES OVER
(abbreviated slip 2 tog, K1, P2SSO)

Slip two stitches together as if to **knit** *(Fig. 6a)*. Knit the next stitch. With the left needle, bring the 2 slipped stitches over the stitch just made *(Fig. 6b)* and off the needle.

Fig. 6a

Fig. 6b

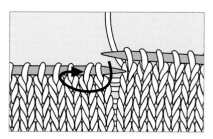
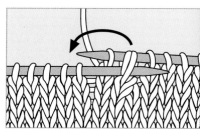

PURL 3 TOGETHER *(abbreviated P3 tog)*

Insert the right needle into the **front** of the first three stitches on the left needle as if to **purl** *(Fig. 7)*, then **purl** them together as if they were one stitch.

Fig. 7

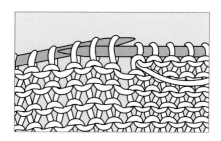

YARN INFORMATION

The Blankets in this book were made using Medium Weight Yarn. Any brand of medium weight yarn may be used. It is best to refer to the yardage/meters when determining how many balls or skeins to purchase. Remember, to arrive at the finished size, it is the GAUGE/TENSION that is important, not the brand of yarn.

For your convenience, listed below are the specific yarns used to create our photography models.

LACE STITCH
Caron® One Pound
#0501 White

BASKET WEAVE
Red Heart® Soft Baby Steps®
Green - #9620 Baby Green
Yellow - #9200 Baby Yellow
Blue - #9800 Baby Blue
Pink - #9700 Baby Pink

LACY RIPPLES
Red Heart® Soft Baby Steps®
Variegated - #9930 Binky Print
Green - #9620 Baby Green
Yellow - #9200 Baby Yellow

LACE CHEVRONS
Red Heart® Super Saver®
Yellow - #0235 Lemon
Green - #0672 Spring Green
Variegated - #0994 Banana
Berry Print

PRIMARY STRIPES
Red Heart® Classic™
White - #0001 White
Blue - #0849 Olympic Blue
Green - #0676 Emerald
Yellow - #0230 Yellow
Orange - #0253 Tangerine
Red - #0902 Jockey Red

RIBBED CHEVRON
Caron® Simply Soft®
#9610 Grape

RECTANGLES
Bernat® Waverly Baby
#55128 Peek-A-Blue

STACKED CABLES
Lion Brand® Pound of Love®
#102 Bubble Gum

We have made every effort to ensure that these instructions are accurate and complete. We cannot, however, be responsible for human error, typographical mistakes, or variations in individual work.

Production Team: Writer/Technical Editor - Linda A. Daley; Editorial Writer - Susan Frantz Wiles; Senior Graphic Artist - Lora Puls; Graphic Artist - Becca Snider Tally; Photo Stylist - Christy Myers; and Photographer - Mark Mathews.